WAYLAND

Published in paperback in 2017
Copyright © Hodder and Stoughton 2017

Wayland
An imprint of
Hachette Children's Group
Part of Hodder & Stoughton
Carmelite House
50 Victoria Embankment
London EC4Y 0DZ

Editor: Debbie Foy
Design: Rocket Design (East Anglia) Ltd
Illustration: Alan Irvine

British Library Cataloguing in Publication Data
Barnham, Kay,
History. -- (Truth or busted)
1. History--Miscellanea--Juvenile literature.
2. Common fallacies--Juvenile literature.
I. Title II. Series III. Foy, Debbie.
902-dc23
ISBN: 978 0 7502 7913 0

Printed in Great Britain by CPI Group (UK) Ltd.
Wayland is a division of Hachette Children's Group,
an Hachette UK company
www.hachette.co.uk

All illustrations by Shutterstock, except 4, 15, 26-27, 41, 53, 55 and 56.

Read this bit first...!

The past is a strange and mysterious place, packed with stuff that sounds so totally *mad* that it's hard to believe it's true. Except, some of this stuff may not be true...

Would His Royal Highness prefer hot water or cold?

Long ago, there was no internet, no Facebook, no Twitter, no email and definitely no ten o'clock news on the television. So if something newsworthy happened — like maybe a blood-crazed despot sticking his enemies on spikes and waiting for them to sink to their deaths — the only way that the world found out the news was if someone witnessed the event and told someone else about it. That someone would tell someone else. And so on. The only problem was that these stories might change a tiny bit as they were passed on, like a sort of ancient Chinese whispers. And because there was no Google in the Middle Ages either, there was no easy way of checking if a story was true or not. Tricky, huh?

Here's a quick quiz. Using your skill and judgement (and not the internet), try to guess whether the following bizarre statements are true or false:

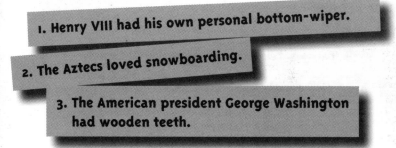

1. Henry VIII had his own personal bottom-wiper.

2. The Aztecs loved snowboarding.

3. The American president George Washington had wooden teeth.

Here's a shocker. All might sound bonkers, but one of the above is 100% true. Here's another shocker — you're going to have to read the book to find out which one that is. Ha ha!

Prepare to travel back into the mists of time and be stunned and amazed by what did and didn't happen there. Things you always believed to be true might be blown out of the water. Kaboom! Things that sound unbelievably disgusting might actually be true. Eww... Discover the deadliest jobs in history and the ancient peoples most likely to chop off your head. Famous words they never said? Check. Ye olde celebrity gossip? That's here too. And much, much more...

read on!

So you might hear myths like...

> ## The Titanic was unsinkable!

Well, that's what everyone thought before 15 April 1912.

★ And the truth is...

Titanic hit an iceberg on her maiden voyage between Southampton and New York City and plummeted to the bottom of the Atlantic Ocean. Of the 2,223 people on board, a staggering 1,517 died. This was mostly because of the bone-chilling seawater, which could kill a swimmer in fifteen minutes flat, but also because there weren't enough lifeboats. And *Titanic* sank so quickly — in just two hours and 40 minutes — that there wasn't time for rescuers to reach the scene and save more people.

What *Titanic*'s owners and builders actually said was that their ship was '*practically* unsinkable', which is like saying they were 99.9% sure that it wouldn't sink, but couldn't totally guarantee it. Unfortunately, the ship became known as the Unsinkable Titanic, making them look very stupid indeed when it *did* sink.

Verdict:  **BUSTED**

6

Totally true Titanic facts

It was the first ship to have a heated swimming pool.

On their final evening, first-class passengers dined on oysters, roast squab, chocolate eclairs and seven other delicious courses.

Less than a minute elapsed between the first sighting of the iceberg and the impact.

The Black Death killed half of Europe!

The Black Death was another name for the bubonic plague — a highly infectious disease carried by rats and fleas — that swept across Europe in 1348.

The plague was a seriously nasty way to die. The symptoms were painful swellings, called buboes. Victims also suffered from fever, vomiting, aches and pains, delirium and extreme sleepiness. It was called the Black Death because the skin around a bubo turned red, then purple and finally black.

Most who caught the Black Death were dead in days.

★ And the truth is...

There are no exact figures for the Black Death, but some historians think that the European mortality rate was about 50%. That's millions of people.

Verdict: **TRUTH** (approximately)

CELEBRITY GOSSIP

from long ago

Did you know that the famous playwright William Shakespeare wrote 37 plays and 154 sonnets, but couldn't spell his own name? Or perhaps his handwriting was so bad that no one could read it properly. Whatever, Shakespeare wasn't very consistent. Here are just a few of the many imaginative and bizarre ways he wrote his surname:

★ Shakespeyre

★ Shackper

★ Shappere

★ Shaxpeer

★ Shakysper

★ Shaxspere

★ Shaxberd...

★ Shexpere

You get the idea. There isn't room to list them all here, but there are at least another 70 variations. And it's not entirely clear if he ever spelt it 'Shakespeare'...

In a gold rush, everyone was a winner!

Why else would gold prospectors spend years digging or crouched over a stream panning, if it wasn't because of guaranteed gold at the end of it?

Gold was discovered in California in 1848 and during the next seven years, about 300,000 prospectors from all around the world rushed there. (Because it was a gold rush. Get it?) But it was a hazardous journey by sea or by land. Those who made it to California found that panning for gold was tough work. Meanwhile, the poor Native Americans lost out big time when their land was overrun with prospectors.

And the truth is...

A very few prospectors *did* find enough gold to become stinking rich and some were lucky enough to make a small profit. But many gold prospectors spent more money rushing to the gold fields than they ever made from the gold they found there.

Verdict: ── **BUSTED** ──

HOW TO BE A GOLD PROSPECTOR

1 Get yourself a gold pan (not a saucepan and definitely not a frying pan — these are quite different).

2 Scoop up gravel from the bottom of a stream, preferably one glistening with golden nuggets.

3 Shake the gold pan under the water. The heavy gold will sink to the bottom of the pan and the lighter sand will float to the top. Like magic! (Except more like science, really.)

4 Swoosh water to and fro over the gold pan so that the sand is washed away, leaving the lovely, shiny gold behind.

5 Sell the lovely, shiny gold.

6 Become horribly rich*.

*If you are very lucky.

Things they never said

'Elementary, my dear Watson.'

This is probably one of Sherlock Holmes' most famous lines. But it doesn't appear in any of Sir Arthur Conan Doyle's novels about the fictional detective.

The Hundred Years' War was exactly a hundred years long

Imagine that. A hundred years of non-stop fighting… Except, the Hundred Years' War wasn't just one war, but several battles that took place between the House of Valois (France) and the House of Plantagenet (England).

The English king, Edward III, started it all. When his uncle, Charles IV of France died, he thought that he should become king of France too. But the French wanted Charles' cousin Philip to be king. So they fought. And fought. Again and again and again. When the kings died, it didn't even signal an end to the fighting. Their successors simply carried on the war.

The Battle of Agincourt, starring Henry V, was one of the most famous battles of the Hundred Years' War. But there were many more. And by the time it was over, Edward III had been dead for 76 years.

Who won? The French. When the war was over, the English had lost all of their French territory apart from the port of Calais.

⭐ And the truth is...

The Hundred Years' War lasted from 1337 to 1453, which made it 116 years long. So, unless you have a very dodgy calculator, the Hundred Years' War... um... wasn't. In fact, it was a name thought up by historians, who presumably couldn't add up, much later.

Verdict: __ **BUSTED** __

CELEBRITY GOSSIP
from long ago

Napoleon Bonaparte (1769–1821) is famous for being a French emperor and a great military leader. But he was also rumoured to be a very short man. (So what? His achievements — before the Battle of Waterloo ended his career — were huge!)

Anyway, the story goes that a doctor measured Napoleon's height in 1802 and said that he was 5 feet and 2 inches tall, which is about 1.57 metres. So that's it sorted then. He was really short. But, er, hang on a minute. What about the small matter of the old French inch being just a bit bigger than the standard measurement? When Napoleon's height was measured, a French inch actually equalled 2.7 cm, while a standard inch is just 2.54 cm. This might not sound like much of a difference until his height is converted in metric. Instead of being 1.57 metres tall, his height suddenly rockets to 1.7 metres tall, which is roughly 5 feet 7 inches. So, in fact, three centuries ago, this would have made him taller than average. Which makes the fact that he was short a <u>very</u> tall story.

People used to wash their clothes in wee

Surely not? Just the thought of washing clothes in smelly old wee is enough to make someone wrinkle up their nose. But it's said that in medieval times – and even as far back as the Ancient Romans – people used wee to remove stubborn stains from their clothes.

⭐ And the truth is...

Well, they had to use something, didn't they? Washing powder hadn't yet been invented and wee – or urine, to use its proper name – contains ammonia, which is very good at getting things clean.

In Ancient Rome, launderers left buckets on street corners for passers-by to stop and 'go'. And when they'd collected enough liquid, the launderers diluted it with water, then popped in the clothes and left them to soak. They might even ask a helper or a slave to stomp on the clothes to get them really clean.

Verdict:

A WEE HISTORY OF THE WORLD

1. The Aztecs used wee to disinfect wounds.

Wee is reasonably sterile, so it makes sense. But many experts say that it's really not a good idea and it is actually much better to use antiseptic cream.

2. Wee-soaked cloth makes a fabulous DIY gas mask.

In the First World War, soldiers actually did this if they didn't have a gas mask with them. The urine protected them against a chlorine attack. Phew-y!

3. Wee makes an excellent invisible ink.

Ask any spy (if you can find one, that is) and they'll tell you that wee is far easier to carry than a bottle of invisible ink. A message written in wee can be later revealed by heating up the paper it's written on.

4. Diluted wee is used by art experts to restore old masterpieces.

Ha ha! This is not true (but it sounds good, doesn't it?).

5. Wee is a teeth-whitener.

Forget the cosmetic dentist. Ancient Romans used wee to make their smiles as white and bright as A-list celebrities. Ting!

6. If you pick a dandelion, you will wet the bed.

The green leaves of a dandelion do actually act as a diuretic, which means that they make you wee more. But picking them has absolutely no effect on a person's bladder whatsoever. In fact, Native Americans used dandelion leaves to cure heartburn, indigestion and constipation.

Roman headhunters searched out the top people for the top jobs!

Can you imagine it? Roman recruitment consultants might have looked for the fastest charioteer and the bravest gladiator and tempted them with oodles of gold. Or maybe they might have found a top advisor for Julius Caesar who didn't want to stab him to death (like his real advisors did).

Nice wheels! Ever thought of racing?

★ And the truth is...

Unbelievably, headhunters were people who actually hunted heads. Roman headhunters thought that taking an enemy's head gave them his or her power too. They threw the freshly chopped heads into wells, rivers or streams as offerings to the Roman gods.

Verdict:  BUSTED

Cavemen fought with dinosaurs!

Ask any grown-up (preferably a slightly prehistoric one) and they'll tell you that they've seen stacks of films in which fur-clad cavemen — and cavewomen, too — fought dinosaurs. So this absolutely must be true, because film directors never make anything up.

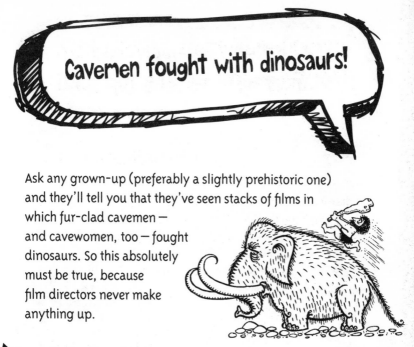

⭐ And the truth is...

This never, ever, ever happened for the simple reason that the last of the dinosaurs lived in the Cretaceous period, while the first humans lived in the Paleolithic Era. And it wasn't as if these chunks of history were a few years or even centuries apart. The last dinosaurs were extinct *65 million years* before the first human appeared on Earth. So there's no way they could have met, let alone fought each other.

Film directors knew this, of course. But they also knew that dinosaurs plus humans equalled a box-office hit, so they bent the truth just a little. And who can blame them.

Verdict: Until time travel is invented

> # Sir Walter Raleigh brought chips (hurray!) and tobacco (boo!) to Europe

One of Elizabeth I's favourite fellows — until he secretly married one of the queen's maids and was banged up in the Tower of London — Sir Walter Raleigh is said to have wowed Ireland with the potato in 1586. It's also said that he stunned the Elizabethan court with the wonders of tobacco smoking. (yeurgh).

★ And the truth is...

Sir Walter Raleigh *did* travel to the New World*, with grand plans to colonise parts of North America. But he failed. Some say that he never even visited a potato-growing region, so it would have been pretty difficult for him to bring back a potato plant. And anyway, the Spanish had already done it.

It was the French diplomat Jean Nicot (not Raleigh) who brought tobacco plants from Portugal to France. Everyone was so thrilled with Monsieur Nicot's discovery that they named 'nicotine' after him. (They might not have been quite so thrilled if they'd known how bad for them smoking was.)

Verdict: doubly **BUSTED**

And as for the tale about Raleigh laying his cloak over a muddy puddle so that Queen Elizabeth I didn't get her shoes dirty... that didn't happen either. But he was definitely beheaded in 1618. Ouch.

* It wasn't really a New World, of course. The Americas had been there all the time. It was just that the Europeans had only just discovered them, so they thought they were new.

DEADLY JOBS
in history

Radium Girls

In the USA in the early 20th century, factory workers (mainly young women) painted watch dials with glow-in-the-dark paint. Unfortunately for them, because the paint contained radium, they also painted their fingernails and teeth and licked the paintbrushes to make them easier to use. This was a truly terrible thing to do. Many of the poor girls died from radiation poisoning and have ever since become known as the Radium Girls.

Things they never said

'Not tonight, Joséphine.'

This is what Napoleon Boneparte is supposed to have said to his wife, the Empress Joséphine, when she asked him to spend the evening with her. Except, as the words were first recorded in the early 20th century, and they lived in the 18th and 19th centuries, he probably didn't say anything of the kind. Having said that, the couple did eventually divorce, so maybe someone decided that he must have said it and made it up on Napoleon's behalf...

The Ancient Olympians raced in the nude!

The very first Olympic Games took place in 776 BC.
Dedicated to Zeus, king of the Greek gods, there was only
one event — a running race, but it soon became a major
sporting occasion, including the long jump, javelin,
discus, wrestling, boxing and chariot racing.
But forget technical sportswear. Sporty types
in Ancient Greece competed in their birthday
suits — they wore *nothing at all*.

★ And the truth is...

Ancient athletes really *did* compete naked, but
no one is entirely sure why. One theory is that a
runner's loincloth slipped and he tripped,
so clothes were considered a safety
hazard and removed. Others think that
the Greeks just liked the human body
— there are plenty of scantily clad
statues, after all — and wanted
to admire the sportsmen as they
competed. It might have been
a tribute to the gods. Or perhaps

ATHENS

it was just because the weather was hot. Whatever the reason, this was something that just the male athletes did. Women did not compete and married women weren't even allowed in the stadium to be spectators.

Verdict: _____ _____

Five more Ancient Olympic truths

1. Boxers were allowed to carry on biffing and bashing their opponents, even after they were down and out.

2. Ancient Olympian runners did not get on their marks before a race. They stood up very straight, with their arms stretched out in front of them.

3. The hoplitodromos event was not a tongue-twister game but a running race in which a competitor ran in full battle gear (including armour and shield).

4. The winner of an event was presented with an olive branch, not a gold medal. Wow.

5. The last Ancient Olympics took place around the 4th century AD. Fans then had to hang on another 1,500 years for the Modern Olympics to begin. They must have been dead tired of waiting.

off with their heads!

Throughout history, some people have made a habit of removing other people's heads. It's not pretty and it's not clever and it's definitely not something you should try at home. (Or not at home. Or anywhere, actually.)

No.1 CELTS

Celts cut off their enemies' heads because they thought that's where the person's soul lived. Afterwards, they dangled the heads from their horses' necks, presumably just to show off.

Sir Isaac Newton discovered gravity when an apple fell on his head

It's a lovely story and it goes something like this...

Once upon a time, Sir Isaac Newton was leaning against a tree and pondering the laws of physics, when suddenly an apple fell from the tree above him and landed on his head. *Bop*. 'Goodness gracious me,' thought Newton, rubbing his crown. 'If gravity can make an apple fall from a tree to the ground, perhaps it works over greater distances — maybe as far away as the Moon? Wow. I must think of a theory to explain that.'

So he did. And he called it Newton's law of universal gravitation.

The End.

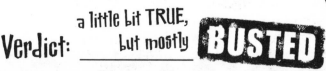

⭐ And the truth is...

A piece of fruit never fell on Newton's head. But we know that he *did* watch an apple fall from a tree, and that this made him think about gravity, because he told people about it. And he did come up with his law of universal gravitation. So whether the apple fell on his head or not doesn't matter. It still made him think.

Verdict: a little bit TRUE, but mostly **BUSTED**

CELEBRITY GOSSIP
from long ago

Julius Caesar was born by Caesarean section

A Caesarean section is an operation performed on a pregnant woman, usually when a natural birth would put her or the unborn baby at risk. A cut is made in the woman's abdomen, the baby is pulled out and the woman is stitched up, as good as new. (Well, that's the straightforward explanation, anyway. Any surgeon will tell you that it's a bit trickier than that.)

It's often claimed that the operation is named Caesarean because the Roman emperor Julius Caesar was born that way.

But in Roman times, the operation meant certain death for the mother … and Caesar's mother was very much alive after he was born. In fact, she lived long enough to become one of his advisors. ('Caesarean' is more likely to come from the Latin verb *caedere*, which means 'to cut'.)

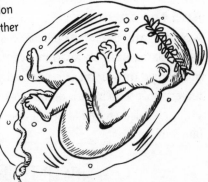

Ancient Egyptians had their noses chopped off if they didn't pay tax!

It seems a pretty extreme punishment for tax evasion, doesn't it? A fine, maybe, but chopping off someone's nose because they didn't pay their taxes sounds *totally* mad.

And the truth is...

Ancient Egyptians whose noses or ears were removed got off lightly. At least they were still alive. Anyone who stole cattle was impaled (see Vlad the Impaler on pages 58-59 for a bloodthirsty explanation of what *this* was) and then his wife and children were forced into slavery. As for grave robbers, they were tortured or killed. It was up to the pharaoh to decide whether they would be drowned, beheaded or burned alive. Goodness, he was spoilt for choice.

Verdict:

Ferdinand Magellan was the first person ever to sail around the world.

The Portuguese explorer didn't set sail with the idea of travelling all around the world — he was actually trying to locate the Spice Islands in Indonesia. In 1519, Magellan left Spain to begin his momentous voyage. The five ships under his command sailed across the Atlantic but the journey became tough. Supplies were low and the crew began to starve. When they landed in the Philippines, disaster struck. Ferdinand Magellan became involved in a battle between local tribes — and was killed.

★ And the truth is...

The *Victoria* was the only one of the original five ships to circumnavigate the globe, but when it arrived back in Spain, Magellan wasn't on it. In fact, only 18 of the original crew were on board.

Verdict: __BUSTED__

Four fab things named after Magellan

Poor Magellan didn't make it all the way around the world, but he might have been pleased to know that after his untimely death a lot of stuff was named after him.

1. Magellanic penguin

Or, as experts (who love complicated words) like to call it, *Spheniscus magellanicus*. This beautiful penguin, which can be recognised by its stripes, lives in the...

2. ...Strait of Magellan

This is a sea route that wriggles between the South American mainland and the archipelago of Tierra del Fuego. It's a great short cut and it was navigated by Magellan in 1520.

3. Magellan spacecraft

In 1989, this space probe became the very first to be launched from the Space Shuttle while it orbited Earth. Its mission was to map the surface of Venus. And it did.

4. Magellanic Clouds

They look like tiny clouds in the night sky, but they're not. The Magellanic Clouds are actual, true-life dwarf galaxies. And they too are named after Ferdinand Magellan.

F. Magellan

You can go around the world in a hot-air balloon in 80 days!

In the 19th century, Phileas Fogg the Victorian adventurer set off on an amazing voyage, to travel around the world in 80 days by rail, steamer, elephant and sledge*, and arriving back in London just before the deadline to claim his reward.

All good so far, except ... Phileas Fogg wasn't real. He's pure fiction – a character invented by French sci-fi author Jules Verne, whose book *Around the World in Eighty Days* became a bestseller when it was published in 1873.

So if it doesn't take 80 days, how long *does* it take to travel around the world?

And the truth is...

In 1870, US businessman George Francis Train travelled around the globe in 80 days. It's very likely that Jules Verne read about this in the newspaper. And in 1872, he may also have seen an advert for travel agent Thomas Cook's more leisurely round-the-world trip that lasted about seven months – and presumably also allowed travellers a little time to sightsee along the way. So Verne knew the journey could be done in 80 days and he also knew that people were growing more interested in world travel. If he were still alive, he'd also know that it's now possible to fly around the world in a passenger jet in just over two days.

* But not balloon, which is the mode of transport most usually associated with Fogg.

Verdict: **BUSTED**

Things they never said

'I see no ships.'

This is what Admiral Lord Nelson, the famous sea captain is supposed to have said at the Battle of Copenhagen in 1801. It wasn't looking good for Nelson and one of his commanders sent a signal for him to withdraw. But Nelson thought they could win. So he raised a telescope to his right eye – the one that hadn't worked since another battle in 1794 – and said, 'I have only one eye. I have a right to be blind sometimes. I really do not see the signal.' They carried on fighting and Nelson's fleet won.

Thomas Crapper invented the flushing toilet

Thomas Crapper was a British sanitary engineer who owned his very own toilet company. He was so successful that he supplied toilets — with cedarwood seats — to kings. And with a name as wonderful as Crapper, people automatically thought that he must have invented the toilet too.

★ And the truth is...

Although he held patents* for many lavatorial inventions, including the floating ballcock, Thomas Crapper didn't invent the flushing toilet. That happened thousands of years earlier in the Bronze Age. Evidence of ancient flushing-toilet systems has been discovered in both the Indus Valley — modern-day Pakistan and northwest India — and the Orkney Islands in Scotland. They must have been flushed with success.

* When an invention has been registered by the inventor, who is then the only person who can make and sell it.

Verdict: **BUSTED**

Loos in History

The Garderobe

This was a medieval toilet in a castle — a tiny room in which there was a hole. This led not to sewers, but straight out into the fresh air. Waste simply fell through the hole and dribbled down the outside of the castle wall. Ewww.

The Common Jakes

This was the name of Henry VIII's massive 28-seater toilet at Hampton Court. Of course, he didn't use it himself. Instead, the king used...

The Closed Stool

Henry VIII had a particularly beautiful toilet, with a padded seat for his royal bottom. It was decorated with so many gilt nails that it must have looked golden. It didn't flush, but that was OK because kings and queens employed someone else to empty their toilet for them.

The Outside Loo

Even during the last century, which isn't that long ago, many people used an outside loo, which was usually in their back yard. But it got pretty cold in winter, which is why (particularly at night-time) many preferred to use...

A Chamber Pot

This was a container that went under the bed — a sort of mini portable toilet. There was no flush, of course. So by the morning, it could get very smelly.

THE GARDEROBE

The weather forecast said there would be sudden showers...

41

The Aztecs loved bungee jumping!

Bungee jumping is not for the faint-hearted*. Fans of this extreme sport launch themselves from bridges, cranes and sometimes helicopters, with their feet tied to a long elastic cord. They fall ... and then *boing* upwards ... and then fall again. This goes on until there is no bounce left in the cord.

So how did the Aztecs have the technology to make an elastic cord made of multiple strands of elastic and covered with polypropylene? They must have been light years ahead of other ancient peoples when it came to science.

★ And the truth is...

The Aztecs *did* bungee jump! But for them, it was a ceremony, not an extreme sport. In the Flying Men Dance, five brave souls climb to the top of a 30-metre pole and then four jump into the air (on the end of ropes). The fifth stands atop the pole and plays musical instruments as the pole slowly rotates, lowering the four flyers to the ground. It's much slower and more tuneful than modern bungee jumping. And amazingly, it's still done today.

* The author would not do this if you paid her a gazillion pounds.

Verdict: **BUSTED**

Queen Victoria wore black for 39 years

When Alexandrina Victoria became queen in 1837, she was just 18 years old. Two years later, she married her sweetheart — and her cousin — Prince Albert, who became the Prince Consort. They had a very happy marriage and nine children. But in December 1861, tragedy struck when the Prince Consort died. Queen Victoria was totally grief-stricken. In keeping with tradition, she immediately put away all of her grand, colourful dresses *forever*. And then she began to wear black.

★ And the truth is...

Queen Victoria went on wearing black — and on and on. In fact, so sad was she about Albert's death that she wore black until she herself died in January 1901.

Verdict:

Lewis Carroll's 'Mad Hatter' is based on fact

The Mad Hatter from *Alice's Adventures in Wonderland* is totally, definitely 100% mad. But did Lewis Carroll — who wrote the book — base his character on real hatters? They can't all have been mad, surely?

★ And the truth is...

A hatter is someone who makes hats, who is also known as a milliner. In the past, a lot of hats were made from felt — a type of woollen material. Instead of being woven like other fabrics, felt is pressed and matted. But in the 18th and 19th centuries, another ingredient was used in the felt-making process. And that was mercury.

Mercury — also known as quicksilver — is used in thermometers, barometers and many other devices. It's a very useful chemical, but it's a very poisonous one too. Sadly, in the 18th and 19th centuries, no one knew this. After breathing in mercury fumes day after day, workers in hat factories were unaware that they were v-e-r-y s-l-o-w-l-y being poisoned.

The symptoms of mercury poisoning include impaired sight and vision, tingling or numb skin, depression, tremors and hallucinations*. But doctors didn't realise that mercury was to blame and simply thought that the hatters had gone mad.

Verdict: **TRUTH** (a bit)

*Seeing things that aren't actually there.

A vomitorium was a handy place for Romans to, um ... vomit

Bleurgh. It's enough to make your stomach churn. Centuries ago, rich Romans gorged themselves on dubious delicacies such as songbirds, ostrich brains and sows' udders, until they were fit to burst. But then, it's said that instead of pushing away their plates and saying, 'Goodness, I'm full,' the Romans simply popped along to the vomitorium. There, they could be spectacularly sick in private, before going back to the dining room and continuing with their feast. Or so the story goes...

★ And the truth is...

Romans headed for the vomitorium *not* when they were feeling a bit green, but when they wanted to make a swift exit. Vomitoria — the word for more than one vomitorium — were nothing to do with vomiting. They were actually passages designed to allow the speedy, efficient emptying of an amphitheatre after a performance.

Verdict:

Cleopatra had a beard

Cleopatra VII (69–30BC) was the last pharaoh of Ancient Egypt, famous for her beauty, her men (Julius Caesar and Mark Antony), and her suicide by asp-bite*. Shakespeare wrote a play about her; Hollywood made films about her. But did one of ancient history's most beautiful women really have a beard?

★ And the truth is...

In Ancient Egypt, it was traditional for pharaohs to wear a false beard as a symbol of their power. Tutankhamun's death mask had a very ornate, very long beard. And it wasn't just the male pharaohs that wore them. Ancient statues of Hatshepsut, another female pharaoh, show her wearing a beard too. So Cleopatra probably *did* have a beard, but it would have been fake and she would only have worn it on special occasions, to show who was in charge.

Verdict:

* See pages 60-61.

In the Middle Ages, everyone thought the world was flat.

It is said that the famous explorer Christopher Columbus struggled to win approval for his first voyage in 1492 because people believed the world was flat — and that he would simply sail off the end of it. Splosh!

⭐ And the truth is...

A *very* long time ago many people *did* think that our planet was flat. But as early as the 6th century BC, the Greek mathematician Pythagoras had begun to suspect that Earth was spherical. The idea caught on. And by the time that Columbus was thinking of sailing across the Atlantic Ocean, most people knew that the world was round.

Verdict: **BUSTED**

Did you know...?

- Amazingly, despite all evidence to the contrary (including photos taken by spacecraft orbiting around our planet) some people still think that Earth is flat. They belong to the Flat Earth Society. Presumably, they have never been on a world cruise.

- Earth is an oblate spheroid, which means that it's like a slightly flattened ball. So it might not be a perfect sphere, but it's definitely not flat.

George Washington had wooden teeth

The first president of the USA suffered from many serious diseases, including smallpox, dengue fever and malaria.

And he also had a lot of toothache...

This might not have been entirely Washington's fault, but more to do with the treatment he received for his illnesses. Some of the medicine he was given contained mercury, which is poisonous and may have caused healthy teeth to go rotten.

Washington tried to keep his teeth clean with tooth powders and mouthwash, but this didn't help — and the potions he used may even have made his teeth worse. Whatever caused his tooth decay, Washington began losing his teeth when he was in his early twenties. By the time he became president, aged 57, he had only one of his own teeth left.

Just don't ask me to say 'cheese'.

 And the truth is...

George Washington did have false teeth, but there is no evidence that they were made from wood. Wooden teeth were worn in Japan from the 16th century, but Washington never had a set. The president's teeth were actually made from human teeth, horse and donkey teeth, hippopotamus ivory and gold. The upper and lower sets of teeth were held together with bolts, while springs helped them open. They must have been *very* awkward to use and *very* painful to wear. Perhaps this is why Washington always looked so serious in his portraits. It might just have hurt too much to smile.

Verdict: ── **BUSTED** ──

off with their heads!

NO.2 THE ZAPOTECS

The Zapotecs of Central America chopped off the heads of their enemies and victims and displayed the skulls on a large rack called a tzompantli. It looked very like an abacus, but instead of coloured beads, there were skulls skewered on it. It must have made it ever so easy to count them...

CELEBRITY GOSSIP
from long ago

Henry VIII had his own personal bottom-wiper

Well, a king couldn't be expected to wipe his own bottom, could he? Instead, Henry VIII employed the son of a nobleman as the groom of the stool — surely one of the most loathsome jobs in the history of forever. However, this soon became one of the most important jobs, too.

The groom of the stool was responsible for making sure that there was a toilet wherever the king went. And while he was waiting to spruce up the royal rear, he also spent a lot of quality time with the king. He listened to the monarch's innermost secrets and passed on important messages. By the end of the day, he must have been totally *pooped*.

TOOTH TRUTHS

1. The very first false teeth date back to northern Italy in 700BC. They were made from old human or animal teeth, held together by gold wire.

2. Sir Winston Churchill's false teeth were sold for a small fortune at auction in 2011. Well, they did belong to a very famous wartime prime minister. (And they were made of gold.)

3. Archaeologists have found ancient false teeth in Mexico, made from wolf teeth. They must have been a howling success.

4. After the Battle of Waterloo in 1815, people plucked teeth from dead - and sometimes not-quite-dead - soldiers and sold them to dentists. They were extremely popular and became known as Waterloo Teeth.

5. The Japanese invented wooden false teeth.

Marie Antoinette said, 'Let them eat cake.'

When Marie Antoinette, the rich wife of Louis XVI of 18th century France, was told that the peasants didn't have enough bread, it's said that she replied, 'Let them eat cake.' How rude!

⭐ And the truth is...

What Marie Antoinette is actually supposed to have said is, *'Qu'ils mangent de la brioche.'* Brioche is not cake, but a delicious type of bread made with lots of eggs and butter. In the 18th century, there was a French law that declared that if bakers ran out of ordinary bread, they had to sell the more expensive brioche at the same low price as the bread. This was to make sure that they made enough of the cheap bread to go round. So Marie Antoinette may have just been saying that if the bakers had run out of cheap bread, then the French peasants should just buy cheap brioche instead.

But it is doubtful whether Marie Antoinette mentioned brioche at all. The phrase was way older than the queen herself. And as the French had seriously fallen out of love with their royal family, it's unlikely she would have tried to annoy them further with silly suggestions about cake or bread. In fact, the heads of Marie Antoinette and Louis XVI were sliced off by the guillotine in 1793.

Verdict: **BUSTED**

Rumour has it that Vlad the Impaler was Dracula the vampire!

Vlad III ruled southern Romania in the 15th century and was probably one of the cruellest people ever. He is thought to have killed as many as 100,000 people. But it's the way he finished people off that is particularly gruesome. Each victim was sat (or impaled) on a long spike and then left there. Gravity pulled them down, while the spike worked its way upwards until at last it popped out just under their chin. It was a long, slow death. Vlad sometimes impaled a few people at the same time. Just for fun.

After his death, Vlad III became known as Vlad the Impaler. But he did have another name. He was also known as Vlad Dracula — but you can put away the wooden stake and the bunch of garlic. Although Vlad was a nasty piece of work, he was not a vampire. His father Vlad II was known as Vlad Dracul, which means 'Vlad the devil'. So Dracula simply means 'son of the devil'.

However, Vlad *did* have a nasty habit of dunking bread in the blood of his victims and then eating it, which is perhaps what gave Victorian author Bram Stoker the idea for his 1897 novel, *Dracula*.

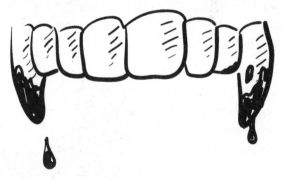

Cleopatra died by asp-bite

Cleopatra famously finished herself off by holding an asp to her skin. When the creature took a bite, she is said to have died from the poisonous venom that flowed into her bloodstream.

★ And the truth is...

According to the great William Shakespeare, this is what Cleopatra is supposed to have said to the deadly asp.

'With thy sharp teeth this knot intrinsicate
Of life at once untie: poor venomous fool
Be angry, and dispatch.'

But as Shakespeare was basing his story on that of an ancient Greek biographer called Plutarch, it's probably best to rewind time further to find out what he said. And Plutarch did say that Cleopatra suffered death-by-asp. Except... Plutarch lived 130 years after Cleopatra died. So how would he know what happened? In fact, there's a whole range of explanations as to how and why Cleopatra died and not all of them to do with venomous snakes.

In 2010, a German historian called Christoph Schaefer announced that he had read a lot of ancient texts and spoken to a lot of toxicologists — experts in poison — and finally he had the answer. Cleopatra had actually died from a mixture of deadly poisons. And not an asp.

Verdict: Probably **BUSTED** though we may never know for sure

So what's an asp anyway?

An asp is simply a venomous snake found in the region of the River Nile. Experts think that the one that was supposed to have chomped on Cleopatra would have been the magnificent Egyptian cobra.

DEADLY JOBS
in history

Gong farmer

Sadly, this was nothing to do with drumming. Or farming. Instead, it was one of the filthiest jobs in the world. Hundreds of years ago, a gong farmer was someone who used to empty cesspits — deep holes in the ground where human waste was stored. The wee would drain away, but the poo would remain and sooner or later it would have to be moved, to make room for more of the stuff. Put simply, gong farmers shovelled poo. Sometimes, they ended up neck-deep in poo, which is where the dangerous part of this job comes in because the fumes that rose from the piles of poo were poisonous enough to suffocate a person. So the job was dirty, smelly and deadly.

POOOOOOO!

The walls of medieval houses were made of cow poo

Ick. Urgh. Gross. Not even the three little pigs made their houses out of cow poo. Surely this is far too disgusting to be true? But take a closer look at some of those pretty Elizabethan houses from the very olden days and you might be surprised.

And the truth is...

The walls *were* made of cow poo, at least partly anyway. There were quite a lot of other ingredients too. Technically, the construction technique is called wattle and daub — it was first used in the Stone Age and has been found in Europe, Asia, Africa and the Americas. Wooden strips are woven together to make a lattice called wattle and this is daubed with a sticky mixture of soil, clay, sand, straw and — hold your nose — animal dung. All gaps in the wattle must be filled to make sure that the wall is solid. Once it's dry, the wattle and daub is often whitewashed to make it more waterproof.

Verdict: 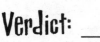 TRUTH

> ## The curse of the Pharaohs means certain death for tomb visitors!

In 1922, archaeologist and Egyptologist Howard Carter and his team discovered the tomb of Tutankhamun in the Valley of the Kings. Their eyes goggled because the tomb was overflowing with ancient treasures. But bad luck followed. Lord Carnarvon, who was funding the excavation, was bitten by a mosquito and died when the wound became infected. One of the team died from fever, one was shot by his wife, one died from blood poisoning and one death was totally unexplained… Within a year, five of those who had witnessed the opening of the tomb were dead. People seriously began to believe that the deaths were all caused by the Curse of the Pharaohs. They had disturbed a mummy's tomb — and they were paying with their lives.

★ And the truth is...

There has never been any actual evidence of a curse inside a pharaoh's tomb. It was all just rumour that was hyped further by the media when Lord Carnarvon died.

But why did so many people die so quickly? It might have been something to do with deadly bacteria contained within the tomb. But it was probably pure coincidence. Perhaps the most compelling evidence that there was never any curse is Howard Carter himself. It is true that he died after the tomb was opened, but it was 17 years later, when he was 64.

Verdict:  **BUSTED**

A pharaoh needed a lot of gear for the afterlife. Here are just a few of the things he or she might take with them:

Food

Jewellery

Combs

Furniture

Pottery bowls

Jars containing their own vital organs

Copper tools

Statues

Magical figurines

Wall paintings

Mummies were embalmed in open-air tents because the whiff was so bad.

If you've ever been on holiday to Egypt, or you know someone who has, you'll also know that it's VERY hot. The same was true in Ancient Egyptian times, which made it rather tricky to prepare a Pharaoh for the afterlife without the dead body ponging a bit. OK, a lot. To make it more pleasant for the embalmer, who had the unenviable job of cutting out the Pharaoh's vital organs and then yanking out the brain through the nose with a hook, they popped him in an open-air tent. Here, the fresh air meant that the body might not smell quite so bad for the 40 days it took to dry out.

Did you know...?

Some Egyptian mummies had onions for eyes! Embalmers took out the eyeballs and replaced them with onions. History doesn't tell us whether they were pickled or not, though these would have stayed fresh longer.

Thomas Edison invented the light bulb

The light bulb was one of the most hotly contested innovations of the 19th century. At one point, it seemed like nearly *everyone* had invented it. And Thomas Edison shouted loudest of all. So was it *really* him who did it?

Before the winner is announced, take a look at the three main contenders for the title of **Inventor of the Light Bulb**.

First up, we have *Humphry Davy*! This brilliant British chemist invented the Davy lamp — an electric lamp that allowed miners to illuminate underground workings without danger of igniting the very flammable methane gas that often caused explosions. It worked by creating a spark between two charcoal rods. He was awarded a medal for his invention in 1816 — hurray! — but it was far too bright and used a lot of power — boo! — which meant that it wasn't much use for everyday use. But Davy deserves bonus points for highlighting the very risky conditions in mines. Bravo!

read on!

Next, step forward *Joseph Swan*! The fabulous British physicist spent years working on his light bulbs, sometimes publishing his findings. And at last, in 1878, he showed off his new light bulb. Its carbon filament — fine thread — glowed brightly, but not for long. So he set about making the light bulb better. But did he finish it in time to win the prize...?

And finally, please give it up for *Thomas Edison*! In 1879, this amazingly entrepreneurial American inventor — who probably had access to Swan's earlier findings — patented his own light bulb. By the following year he had improved this light bulb so much that it glowed for a totally brilliant — *geddit?* — 1,200 hours.

Mr Humphry Davy

...and his lamp

c

e e

b b

g

f

k

Mr Thomas Edison

some old lamp
(but not Edison's)

⭐ And the winner is...

Humphry Davy didn't invent the light bulb, but it was his
lamp that really got things started. And Thomas Edison didn't
invent the light bulb either — Joseph Swan was officially the
Inventor of the Lightbulb — but he did make it much better.
Edison was a businessman as well as an inventor and when
he saw an opportunity for improving something and making
money from it, he went for it. In the end, it didn't really
matter that he didn't win the light-bulb race. He became
very rich anyway.

Verdict: **BUSTED**

Viking chiefs were cremated on their longships

It wasn't just the Viking chief's body that was burned — the longship was piled with stuff that he might need in the next life. This included food, beer, clothes, weapons, jewellery, dogs and horses. Sometimes, even the chieftain's wife or his favourite slave girl went with him. Unfortunately for them, they had to be killed first. Either the woman volunteered or she was dragged to the ship, kicking and screaming.

★ And the truth is...

It sounds a bit extreme, doesn't it? But it's all true. The Vikings believed that a ship would carry the dead safely on their journey to the next life and they gave their chiefs a magnificent send-off.

Viking funerals took place by rivers or near the coast. And then, once the longship was loaded up with bodies and belongings, it was set adrift on the water. A relative of the chief threw the first firebrand and then the other mourners joined in. Blazing brightly, the longship would sail away.

Verdict: _____ TRUTH

Help!

ouch!

AWFUL ANCIENT PUNISHMENTS

The **Vikings** punished murderers by confiscating their land and belongings and then declaring that anyone could kill them — without fear of punishment themselves.

NOOO!

arghh!

Things they never said

'Houston, we have a problem.'

In 1970, the Apollo 13 space mission went spectacularly wrong. An oxygen tank exploded, temperatures plummeted and there was very little power on board the spacecraft. Many believe that when the commander of the spaceflight, Jim Lovell, spoke to mission control in back on Earth, he said, 'Houston, we have a problem.'

The truth is that he actually said, 'Houston, we've had a problem.' (Space fans might like to know that Commander Lovell then said, 'We've had a main B bus undervolt.' This had nothing to do with public transport.) But somehow, no one remembers this. And even if they do, perhaps they actually think that 'Houston, we have a problem' sounds better.

Whatever Apollo 13's problem was, it meant that the moon landing was cancelled. But the good news is that all three astronauts found a way around the problem and made it back to earth safely, splashing down in the Pacific Ocean. And everyone in Houston (and the rest of the world) was delighted.*

*Some of them were so delighted that they made a film called - can you guess? - Apollo 13 in 1995, starring Tom Hanks as Jim Lovell.

The Greeks hid inside the wooden horse of Troy

In Greek mythology, the Trojan War was a long war between Troy and Sparta. It all began because Paris of Troy fell in love with Helen and whisked her away from her husband Menelaus, the King of Sparta (a city state in Greece). Menelaus wanted his wife back, so he gathered an enormous fleet of ships and sailed to Troy to fetch her. But Paris refused to give Helen up, so Menelaus besieged the city.

After ten years and many deaths, the Greeks came up with the brilliant idea of building a huge wooden horse and using it to get inside the sturdy city walls of Troy.

A few soldiers were chosen to hide inside the wooden creature, while the rest of them sailed a short distance away and hid. Thrilled that the Greeks had gone at last, but curious about the enormous horse, the Trojans pulled it inside their city. That night, the Greeks crept out of their hiding place and sailed back to Troy in darkness. They flung open the gates of Troy and rushed inside. The city of Troy was doomed.

★ And the truth is...

No one really knows if the Trojan War ever happened or not. Greek poet Homer wrote about the events in his epic poems the *Iliad* and the *Odyssey*, but this may have been a few hundred years later. Also, the Trojan War is part of Greek mythology. As well as featuring a host of famous names — Paris, Hector, Achilles and Helen, the most beautiful woman in the world — it also starred Greek gods and goddesses too. So the entire war may just have been a story... Except, in 1870, German archaeologist Heinrich Schliemann found the remains of an ancient city that could have been Troy.

So if the city of Troy existed, perhaps the war took place too. Because the Greek city states did have a reputation for war. And if the war took place, perhaps they even had a wooden horse...

but maybe, just maybe, this was the TRUTH...

Verdict: Probably **BUSTED**

AWFUL ANCIENT PUNISHMENTS

In Ancient Greece, children caught stealing were beaten. It didn't matter that they were stealing because they were starving. Under one particular ruler called Draco, nicking an apple meant the death sentence...

DEADLY JOBS
in history

Construction worker on the Burma Railway

The Burma Railway was 415 km long, but so many workers died during its construction that it became known as the Death Railway instead. Asian civilians and Prisoners of War were forced to work in terrible and dangerous conditions. By the time the railway was complete, 106,000 people had died, which meant one death for every 4 metres of track.

EWW, IT CAN'T BE TRUE!

Roman loo paper was a sponge on a stick.

The Ancient Romans had truly magnificent toilets. There were long marble seats, walls decorated with beautiful artwork and running water. Better still, because the public toilets were designed for many people to use them at the same time, the Romans could even chat to a neighbour while they did their business. How convenient. So surely such fabulous loos would have had loo paper to match?

Nope.

Ancient Roman loo paper wasn't on a roll. It wasn't three-ply, four-ply, quilted, velvety or recycled. In fact, it wasn't loo paper at all. It was a spongia — a sea-sponge — on a stick. And if you think that sounds dodgy, it gets worse. They all shared the same sponge.

Gross!

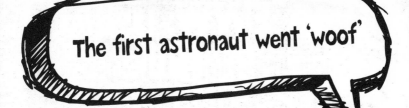

The first astronaut went 'woof'

(And no, this doesn't mean that they went up in flames.)

Ha ha! How totally ridiculous! It sounds like something that would happen in a pantomime. One of the world's great superpowers sent a dog into space? *Oh no, they didn't.*

★ And the truth is...
Oh yes, they did.

In the 1950s, Soviet scientists did not know whether it was possible for a human to survive a launch into space. And as they didn't want to test the theory with a real, live person, they decided to send a dog into space instead. A stray named Laika was chosen for this important job and on 3 November 1957, she rocketed into space on board *Sputnik 2*. Laika became the first creature to go to space and the first to orbit Earth, but sadly she died from overheating after a few hours. In Moscow, there stands a statue of a rocket with a dog perched on top to remember her.

Verdict:

The Wild West was dangerous, violent and very, very wild

In Westerns, that's certainly how it looks — they tell the story of life in the Western USA in the late 19th century. The cowboys in these movies spent most of their time involved in gunfights and saloon shoot-outs. They galloped across prairies, Stetsons pulled low, rifles at the ready. And they were pretty good at sliding drinks along bars without spilling them, too. Sometimes, they even looked after cows. Meanwhile, outlaws wreaked havoc and sheriffs tried to keep the peace. Life was never dull, often dangerous and always exciting.

And the truth is...

Before the moviemakers became
involved, American frontier families
headed out west and life was
very hard. Cowboys
looked after cows,
because that was their
job. It's doubtful whether
many of them lived lives as
daring and glamorous as in the
Westerns — these were mostly
stories dreamed up by Hollywood.
In fact, the most common cause
of death for cowboys was not
gunfights, but horse-riding
accidents.

Gunfights did happen, but
they were rare. The Gunfight
at the OK Corral was one event
that really did take place. It
only lasted 30 seconds, but that
was long enough to kill three outlaws, wound three
other men and give Wyatt Earp the reputation as being the
toughest and deadliest gunman of the Old West. But the truth
is, he probably didn't have that much competition.

Verdict: **BUSTED**

All pirates were men

Pirates ruled the seas in the 18th century. They swashbuckled and swore. They spoke in deep, booming voices, terrifying the poor souls whose galleons they were plundering. So they must all have been men, because this was *hardly* ladylike behaviour.

And the truth is...
Step aside, **Blackbeard**.
Women were just as good
as men at being pirates.

Jeanne de Clisson was
known as the Lioness of
Brittany. She lurked in the
English Channel, laying in wait for warships. But she never killed
everyone on board — she always left two or three sailors alive so
they could tell everyone back at home who had attacked them.

Grace O'Malley was an Irish pirate who was known as the
Sea Queen of Connaught. Her exploits — including theft,
abduction and murder — are legendary.

Then there was **Mary Read**, whose ship was taken over
by pirates in the early 18th century. She became one
of them, sailing the Caribbean with another female
pirate, **Anne Bonny** and Calico Jack, who was all
for equality on the high seas.

Verdict: __ **BUSTED** __

DEADLY JOBS
in history

•WANTED•
Death-cart Labourers

Check out this fabulous 14th century career opportunity! Everyone you know might be dropping dead from the pesky plague, but are you fit and healthy? Do you want to earn very high salary? Can you put up with the stench of rotting flesh? Then come and work as a death-cart labourer! All you have to do is collect plague victims and pop them in a plague pit. It's that easy!

The Small Print
Must be prepared to work night shifts, because no one really wants to see you doing your deathly job, and there's a fairly big chance that you'll catch the plague from all the dead bodies and die a horrible death too, but just think of the money, eh?

EWW, IT CAN'T BE TRUE!

Ancient Greeks and Romans used pig and ox bladders as footballs.

First, they blew the bladder up like a balloon and then they stuffed it with leaves and hair. Unfortunately, these footballs punctured quite easily (so a World Cup squad would have found it very difficult to sign one without bursting it). So now they're made of plastic and rubber, which is way less yucky.

> # Sir Francis Drake was playing bowls when he spotted the Spanish Armada

He was a sea captain, a pirate, a politician, he was knighted by Elizabeth I and, according to legend, he was also as cool as a cucumber when it came to sticky situations. It's said that when the Spanish Armada was spotted off the English coast, Sir Francis Drake was playing a leisurely game of bowls. But rather than spring onto his battleship to repel the enemy, he calmly decided to finish his game. And then trounce the Spanish.

★ And the truth is...

Sir Francis Drake liked bowls, but there's no reliable evidence to show that he was playing the game at the time the Armada appeared over the horizon. And anyway, he wasn't an idiot. He knew that beating 22 galleons and 108 armed ships in battle was more important than winning a game of bowls.

Verdict: Almost certainly  **BUSTED**

Elizabeth I had black teeth!

Urgh. Can you imagine a queen with teeth so rotten that she looked like a Halloween ghoul when she smiled? Surely this must be a myth...

★ And the truth is...

Elizabeth I loved sugary food and hated the dentist, which isn't a good combination now and wasn't in the 16th century either. She and other rich Elizabethans feasted on swan and peacock, followed by fruit pies, cakes, custards and marzipan sweets. (The poor ate a far healthier diet of vegetables.) As she grew older, the queen's teeth went black with decay. The toothache must have been unbearable. But even so, it's said that when Elizabeth went to the dentist to have her rotten teeth pulled out, she was so scared of the pain that one of her advisors had to have one of his own teeth extracted first, to show her how easy it was. Unfortunately, when Elizabeth did have fewer teeth, another problem arose — it became difficult for her to speak *and* for her loyal subjects to understand her.

Anyone fancy a bag of sweets...?

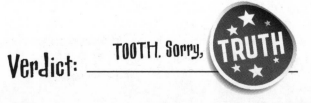

Verdict: TOOTH. Sorry, TRUTH

AWFUL ANCIENT PUNISHMENTS

In Ancient Rome, arsonists were whipped and then set on fire, murderers were sewn into leather sacks and then thrown into a river, traitors were beheaded and those who stole food were sent to work in mines.

DEADLY JOBS
in history

Chimney sweeps

In the film Mary Poppins (1964), chimney-sweeping looks so much fun. But in real life, it was anything but. Before long brushes were invented, chimney sweeps cleaned the chimneys by hand. They would crawl up the chimney, brushing the soot away with a hand brush. Many chimney flues did not go straight up, but bent back and forth, sometimes turning corners on their wiggly way up to the chimneypot. And because some flues were too narrow for a grown-up, the chimney sweep in charge sent children up instead. Chimney sweeps as young as six often got stuck, dying from suffocation, fire or heat. They certainly wouldn't have sung or danced on the rooftops. Well, not before 1875, when the practice was banned forever.

The Boston Tea Party was a tea party. In Boston.

The Boston Tea Party was FABULOUS fun. Imagine an all-American tea party with the biggest cuppas ever. And then forget it, because the only thing that the Boston Tea Party and an actual tea party had in common was wet tea leaves.

And the truth is...

In 1773, a change in the law meant that the British East India Company could export tea to British colonies in the USA and sell it cheaper than the local tea growers. Scared that they might go out of business, the colonists were *not* happy.

When the HMS *Dartmouth* arrived in Boston Harbour, filled to the gunwales with tea, the colonists refused to unload it, ordering the captain to take it back to Britain. But the captain refused to go. Another two ships arrived — HMS *Eleanor* and HMS *Beaver*. They were refused entry too. After a stand-off, a group of colonists crept aboard on 16 December and threw the entire cargoes of all three ships into the waters of Boston Harbor. It was an event that became known as the Boston Tea Party.

Verdict: __ **BUSTED** __

off with their heads!

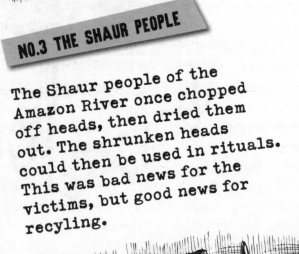

NO.3 THE SHAUR PEOPLE

The Shaur people of the Amazon River once chopped off heads, then dried them out. The shrunken heads could then be used in rituals. This was bad news for the victims, but good news for recyling.

The Vikings wore horned helmets

The Vikings have a reputation for being fierce warriors with a nasty habit of invading other countries. (In fact, 'viking' means pirate raid.) They came from Denmark, Norway and Sweden and from the 8th to the 11th centuries, they travelled to the rest of Europe and beyond, raiding, fighting and settling. So it's not all that surprising that they wore hats decorated with big *scary* animal horns, is it?

★ And the truth is...

They didn't. Horned helmets would have been *rubbish* on the battlefield. As well as being cumbersome and dangerous, they would have provided an excellent handhold for the enemy and before he knew it, the Viking would have been history.

Most Viking warriors actually wore plain conical helmets made of leather and stiffened with wood and metal, while the chieftains wore more protective metal helmets. Apart from some references to Vikings wearing helmets with horns — or antlers or wings — during religious ceremonies, there's no evidence that other Vikings wore them. It was during the 19th century that the idea of horned helmets became popular and is still believed today. You won't find many fancy-dress Vikings *without* horns.

Verdict:  BUSTED

Where can I find myths about...

100%
SUCKER-PROOF

GUARANTEED!

Take a look at our other marvellously mythbusting titles...

Tip:
Turn over!